DARKEND

_hydrus

Published by: Hydrus
Photography by: Hydrus
Proofreading by: Gabrielle G.
Cover Design by: Cleo Moran - Devoted Pages Designs
Formatting by: Cleo Moran - Devoted Pages Designs
https://www.devotedpages.com

Manufactured in the United States of America

ISBN: 978-1-7357824-2-3

HAILEY

DRINK YOUR DARKNESS

I walk without my shadow
your relentless love and kindness
left so much to desire from humanity.

_hydrus

Dedicated to my Dex

DarkEND is a small look into the world I call
my reality. Through poems, photography
and art, I try to capture the ups and downs of
this voyage we call life, and sometimes
I refer to it as just existing.

Embedded in my words are stories of emotions
and feelings that range from the darkest of
moments to times of having some type of hope
for resolve.

Life is raw and ever-evolving, and we always
seem to put ourselves last overall. Time
proves to be quite relentless.

I hope that we all find common ground through
our everyday struggles and in the end,
understand that love, although painful
at times, can provide so many answers.

So the question then becomes
"how can we better love ourselves?"

Write your

Breath has left you
Skin drapes upon frame
Life I once knew
Vanished the flame

Soulless and frozen
Broken and pain
Words without meaning
Memories drain

Sadness engulfs me
Triumphant the loss
Etched is your friendship
Forever my cross

Yearning to hold you
Missing your touch
Wounds never healing
Livings too much

Friend
_hydrus

1

Mages dance
Upon broken skulls
Casting spells
Black nuptials

Bleeding hearts
Feathered manes
Weathered tears
Dust remains

Roaches feast
Dine on sin
Organs ripped
Angels sing

Verdict
_hydrus

Bells swing madly
Marching doves fly
Hooded freaks march
Masked skulls cry

Bloodied sharp steel
Thirsty lips quench
Saints play harps
Wretched fowl stench

Folded eyes uncover
Deathly cheering groans
Faded thoughts encounter
Ruthless piercing stones

Drenched in your vile
Knotted tainted skin
Severed from existence
Angelic moral sin

Confession
_hydrus

Claws buried
Deep within
Torn flesh
Haunted grin

Mangled veins
Bone and dry
Twisted earth
Gaping eye

Toothless gaze
Silent rot
Footsteps drag
Cannot be caught

Lifeless souls
Will betray
Among them
All decay

Gashes
_hydrus

Knife in hand
Second chance
Eyes are closed
New romance

Quiet steps
A crawl or two
Blankets cover
Foolish drool

Pound and batter
Break the skin
No more chatter
From within

Voices
_hydrus

I have spent my life searching for you
        only to spend the rest of it trying to erase you

                                        _hydrus

Can the rain stop
Pounding at my soul
Blinding delight
Shadows control

Merciless thunder
Screams from above
Harpies breathe fire
Sacrificed love

Risen the demon
Mounted on steed
Horned assassin
Roaring speed

Pounding the anvil
Upon shuttering wing
Slicing through bone
Ripping out skin

Gorging on armor
Torn to display
Evil has triumphed
End of all days

Horsemen
_hydrus

Pages turn blindly
Escape from ones greed
Never the truth
Hidden the need

Blood filled letters
Strokes of the mind
Lost emotions
Chapters unkind

Figures run rampant
All through ones eye
Mimic the maker
An endless disguise

Lingering darkness
Blood stained notes
Feeling of weakness
Faltering quotes

Doubting ones being
One must not trust
Eternal denial
Scripted in lust

Author
_hydrus

Broken flower
Hidden from light
Wilting soul
Forsaken plight
Abandoned drowned
All is gone
Shattered petals
Twisted thorns
Decay finds you
Life no more
Buried ashes
Earthly gore

Ashes
_hydrus

Nails scratch upon my back
Quivering rot stench of hack

Worms devour ink filled flesh
Carrions scour butchered mess

Blood stained floors heaving bowels
Adorning filth dirt drenched towels

Walking corpse death once bled
Sliced and shredded severed head

Solitary
_hydrus

Running toward knowing
Life has finally left
Tears and screams follow
I silently wept

End had come slowly
Devoured the host
Murdered in darkness
Shattered the ghost

Body laid silent
Heart is now torn
Forever lay dormant
No soul to mourn

Gone
_hydrus

I had to go through your hell to reach my heaven
watch me fly as I watch you burn

_hydrus

Skeletal limbs
Adorn the road
Crows on branches
Murders row

Hooks in jaw
Quiet noise
Padded walls
Rubber toys

Voices whisper
Many names
Jumping moods
Serrated veins

Almost lost
Someone lied
At what cost
Puddles cried

Convicted
_hydrus

Savage steps
Attract a look
Yearning lips
On the hook

Tempted fate
Drew her in
Hunger came
Hard within

Fingers grab
Pull in close
Flesh aroused
Take in host

Pounding skin
Beating heart
Grinding bones
Naked art

Encounter
_hydrus

Neon lights
Flutter like flies
Drinks are empty
Distant cries
Canvas sky
Brushed in black
Dotted eyes
Easy snack
Shattered dreams
Painted face
Weathered smoke
Torn up lace
Watchers peer
On demand
Mirrored walls
Unwanted hand
Powdered lines
Faded ink
Lost dreams
Broken sink
Sun has risen
Life is night
Broken bones
Darkened light

Slave
_hydrus

Mounted beast
Armored back
Soldiers fall
Under attack
Fire burns
Bodies lay
Under oaks
To decay
Savage brothers
Side by side
Dragons breath
Beaten life
Embers glare
Flesh will burn
Royal crowns
Once adorned
Severed limbs
Scattered bones
Valiant tales
Treasure stones
Creatures reign
Bloodied fields
Foggy lands
Tattered shields
Battled princes
Twisted fates
Those who live
Hell awaits

Impaled
_hydrus

Tattered rose
Stolen rage
Battered soul
Inner pain

Fearful son
Hidden past
Broken arm
Bandaged cast

Gun in hand
Twisted fate
Trigger pulled
It's too late

Even
_hydrus

Love Your

Beautiful

_hydrus

Here you lay broken
In my arms you cry
Heartbeat slowly fading
Raindrops fall from sky

Where did we go wrong
How much I let you down
Painful nights so long
Want to sink and drown

No more lies or stories
Will live with the deceit
Guilty deeds not worry
Forever you will sleep

Cheated
_hydrus

Thorny vine
Tangled soul
Tightening
Take control

Trapped inside
Taunted fate
Terrified
Tortured state

Twisting stem
Tricked to grow
Tainted
True sorrow

Tulip
_hydrus

Withered time
Dragging on
Helpless path
Shrieking song

Sluggish pain
Pounding turn
Idled hands
Constant burn

Flames take hold
Bells begin
Truth for told
Eternal sin

Damned
_hydrus

Mangled hair
Bed sheets thrown
Pillows hide
Shredded gown

Lip red blush
Pounding flesh
Bodies crushed
Moaning hushed

Wetness sweat
Feelings kept
Desire felt
As I knelt

Taken
_hydrus

Grayish brow
Saddened tone
Loss of soul
Frantic groan

Yells and screams
Wounded bones
Lay upon
Granite stones

Exiled
_hydrus

Tempt fate by being who you truly are

_hydrus

Lost in your words
Painted mazes
Smoke filled rooms
Sexy phrases

Undressed thoughts
Closing eyes
Wanting you
Butterflies

Lips on skin
Passions brew
Hunger stings
Is it true

Delusion
_hydrus

You left my life too soon

Never to return for a kiss

I am empty without you

Lost

Echoes of your voice still linger
Visiting me in my dreams

My sadness is so deafening
Words simply do not matter

Marooned
_hydrus

Losing my mental state
The veil of loneliness lingers
Hungering for a solemn mate
Chains link quiet dangers

Visions rampantly run
Knowingly forcing my senses
Nocturnally the beast has sung
Death to consequences

Hunted
_hydrus

Winter came in spring
When my flower past
Wilted from disease
Weathered and cast

Will I remember
Willows in the bloom
Wanting forever
Wasted life too soon

was
_hydrus

Shady blue eyes glaring
Hidden by silk and sheet
Warm soft skin is moving
Reaching for flesh beneath

Pouty lips upon me
Tracing every hard inch
Bodies moving tightly
Fingers grabbing pinch

Piercing and thrusting heat
Arched and twisted desire
Twisted souls cannot breathe
Quenching ones inner fire

Morning
_hydrus

Do not question your purpose
when those around you are lost
_hydrus

Black lips
Find my skin
A tender kiss
Love within

Fingertips
Caress my brow
Hands on hips
In the now

Neck back
Throat exposed
No more mask
No more clothes

Nails scratch
Streak and tear
Exposed skin
So unaware

Passions rough
Lust divine
Captured trust
Forever mine

Darken Hall
_hydrus

A stolen kiss taken
Angelic wings broken
Passions were forsaken
The lust was awakened

Guilt
_hydrus

Lost in a moment
Feeling alive
Forgotten times
Our path revived

A rewind on life
Emotions so real
Love again stolen
Begin the ordeal

Fate
_hydrus

Time stood still
That sunny day
Thoughts of you
Turned all gray

Torn from me
Twilights game
Terribly
Tomorrow came

Thoughtless
_hydrus

Broken soul
Washed upon rocks
Forbidden trust
Betrayed words
Moaning song
All is lost
Life gone wrong
At what cost

Tested
_hydrus

Your touch makes me forget I am broken

Your lips make me remember I am alive

_hydrus

Tightly gripped
Held so firm
Pressing on me
Clothes are torn

Kissing lips
Devouring lust
In your arms
I solely trust

Safe
_hydrus

Infectious smile
Detains to control
Spells again casted
Upon my dark soul

Brightness crashes
Shining black light
Covering gashes
Selfish delight

Treacherous creature
Deceptive you are
Changing true nature
Bounding my scars

Ousted for treason
Trusted liar of shame
Banished you will be
Extinguished the flame

Manipulated
_hydrus

Deceptive creature
Lurking around
Venomous hissing
Purpose profound

Silently coiled
Poised to fight
Deceitfully spoiled
Forbidden a bite

Lured by indulgence
A virginal tear
His motives sinful
Her weakness clear

A Taste
_hydrus

Painful to watch you cry
Tears falling want to die
Streams flowing from your eyes
Feeling worried can't reply

Helpless
_hydrus

Who can hurt you this way
Helpless feelings far away
Never knowing what to say
Must live another day

Who Are You
_hydrus

Don't search
    for what you never lost
                              _hydrus

An existing pretender
Manipulated with lies
Hiding from emotions
Evading the disguised

Questioning ones worth
Purpose to still believe
Silence strongly put forth
Empty sadness received

Cries for honest answers
Path to be carefully taken
Quickly extinguished reason
Actions loudly mistaken

Illusions of true passion
Faded and devoured
Never to take action
Sentenced as a coward

Snared
_hydrus

Withered and frail fractured dove
Society has you battered
Pelted by judgments cruel hate
All your brittle bones shattered

Underestimated strength
Unvalued worth to exist
Against all hidden masses
The individual persists

Fearlessly spreading your wings
Proving all at fault and wrong
All the hearts smirkingly pierce
Deafening them with your song

Fly
_hydrus

You stole my breath
Upon a simple gaze
A textured flower
My distracted haze

Beauty solely owned
In a garden of weeds
Wondrous in growth
Unique from a seed

Cloaked in your vines
Light cannot break
Soul made invited
Darkened your mistake

Beware
_hydrus

Passion awake
Chains untangle
Owner buried
Cravings ravel

Distant menace
Pains not expired
Untangled webs
Flaming desire

Deprived from joy
Emerged to lust
Drenched in new bliss
From the first thrust

Awakening
_hydrus

Wounded flower
Rooted in mistrust
Wilting forward
Stepped on and crushed

Clouds will reopen
Dispatching down tears
Witnessing your rise
Drowning your fear

Rains
_hydrus

Only your dreams
        reflect the true desires that
your heart can never obtain
                                _hydrus

Poisoned strain
Fluidly dripping
Tainted tongue
Chatter seeping

Relentless banter
Jawing misdeeds
Zealous in nature
Burying the seed

Nurturing doubt
Festering sin
Coaxing to spout
Venomous grin

Slither
_hydrus

Panicked in my loss
Frantic feelings capture
Buried with this cross
Encaged senses rapture

Darkness solely reigns
Forbidden passion lurks
Wounded unhinged pain
Revengeful actions smirk

Mazes of emotion
Grounded in true sadness
Demons cause commotion
Blackened with my madness

Voiceless screams are running
Clawing at each door
Empty answers calling
My sentence evermore

Committed
_hydrus

Troubled journey
Misguided fate
Deceived venture
Plagued state

Roaming glance
Romantic spell
Captured trance
New found hell

Reluctant partner
Damaged soul
Silent anger
Feared control

Mislead
_hydrus

Vacant eyes glistened
Sounds ceasing to be
Finally life has left you
Buried with your dreams

Dimmed
_hydrus

Embedded kisses burning
Saliva eating flesh
Polluted mouth is spewing
Infested human wretch

Black flies slowly feasting
On tasteless uttered sounds
Suspicious words are seeping
Filth lacing every sound

Stranded with this being
Witness to constant lies
Deception always haunts me
Slashes will paralyze

The Plot
_hydrus

Morning light settles
Sheets begin to peel
Eyes begin to hunt
Hands grabbing to feel

Devoured by flesh
Craving my descent
Buried in passion
Tasting all your scent

Legs quickly wrapping
Anchor to my skin
Pulling bodies close
Lunging into sin

Hunger
_hydrus

Outstretched wondering hands
Devouring embrace
Gorging on wet lips
Drunken sensuous state

Wicked captive stare
Yearning for a taste
Nails ripping to tear
Holding you in haste

Hostage in your arms
Tongue starts to trace
Feasting on your throat
Mouth finds its place

Bitten
_hydrus

Faithful witness
Preying eyes
Scratching lurking
Cunning spy
Haunting horror
In disguise
Superstition
Terrifies
Spirit senses
Nightly cries
Silent servant
Someone died

Familiar
_hydrus

Hair draped skin
Softly soaked
Droplets streaking
Movements evoke

Sensuous lines
Smoothly arouse
Desired stroking
Suggestive browse

Alluring stares
Enticing grins
Fingers calling
Heat within

Quiet intention
Hands roam
Passioned tension
Primal moans

Drenched
_hydrus

Dangerous black rose
Painted leaves of sin
Exhausting scent
Tortured within

Broken and battered
Torn from the earth
Ghostly encounters
Enchanted from birth

Falling in pain
Weathered betrayal
Misunderstood beauty
Chaotically frail

Mystic in nature
Desirable scream
Tender temptation
Unstoppable dream

Intoxicated
_hydrus

Darkness is my brother
Blames me for all misdeeds
Chained by the lies of light
On judgments sin he feeds

Kin
_hydrus

Faded memory
Haunt my dreams
Blurry images
Cannot see

Distant voices
Muted smiles
Songs so distant
Infantile

Cannot believe
You are gone
Endlessly
So lonesome

Clouded
_hydrus

Wailing heart
Mourning you
Distance keeps
Love askew
Wishing you
Were with me
Never enough
So patiently
Times our enemy
Always dawn
No chances
Life goes on
Fingers touch
All is felt
Ripped away
Crushed and knelt
Will you return
Or simply go
Wishes forgotten
Answer is no

Refusal
_hydrus

Frost paints the windows
A shiver runs through my veins
Lipstick marks my arm
Abandoned with this cruel pain

Nameless
_hydrus

Visions of corpses
Lined up for a feast
Gorging on veiled lies
Ripping all deceit

Infected hordes hunt
Clawing at my eyes
Blinding all existence
Fear they terrorize

Shadows cannot mask
Intentions of the wicked
Darkness dirty task
Angering the afflicted

Reaper will avenge
Hatred made me whole
Bearing all the blame
Tearing out my soul

Shredded by the blade
Rest will never call
Hunger quickly fades
Punishment for all

Captured
_hydrus

Your castle
        is your armor
your weapon
    is common sense

_hydrus

Her eyes told a story
That her mouth could not speak

Her screams were left unheard
Silenced by the weak

Tears Of A Hostage
_hydrus

Sadness overwhelms
Words escaping reach
Battered circumstance
Berated by my speech

Left and forgotten
Inflicting harsh pain
Felt to be rotten
Feeling so ashamed

Brutally attacked
Body cannot stand
Time has run out
One must take a stance

When the monster sleeps
Hands will overtake
Slicing at his throat
Ending my mistake

Erased
_hydrus

Dark dense solemn slumber
Buried beneath cold sheets
Window pain slams thunder
Quiet breeze glides underneath

Whispers secretly voiced
Familiarly divine
Deeply trance one keeps
Clasping to every sign

Songs faintly calling back
Reaching out dismayed
Woken by confession
Shockingly betrayed

Motive
_hydrus

Masked angels dance on my skull
Angered at my presence
Bloodied trumpets thunderous call
Hatred filled with vengeance

Burning flock set a flame
Judgment for defying
Silent prayers not reclaimed
Hollowed eyes are crying

Fallen
_hydrus

Life seems endless as time
Until it crushes your mind
Resting hopes on the Divine
Answers you cannot find

Search
_hydrus

You are a flower bleeding in a field of thorns

that can only be reached by the light you so selfishly evade

_hydrus

My love was taken
Ripped from my side
Clenched to her soul
Watched as she died

Voiceless regret
Of times never spent
Guilt with denial
A godless lament

No answers to prayers
Solemnly asked
Tortured I paid
For sins from my past

Due
_hydrus

Laughter quietly faded
Touch was a distant glance
Passion was separated
End of a true romance

Lost will be the kisses
Sound of angelic voice
Ripped from me you were taken
Abandoned without a choice

Sudden
_hydrus

My lonely heart
Bleeds sorrow
Abandoned
Forgotten
Beat less slumber
Drained of life
Motionless
Silenced
Only your death
Revives me

Lifeless
_hydrus

Distant heart that beats
Removed from my hands
Left alone to cease
Shocked to understand

Empty voices shriek
Sadness new found home
Hidden to make weak
Madness forced to roam

Have I been deceived
Tricked to let you go
Never to find peace
For this I will owe

Snatched
_hydrus

Happy to discover
A flame has caught your eye
Left me for another
A distant empty cry

Shattered empty questions
A silent fleeting bye
Enraged in my deception
Mindful of the lies

Vengeance will be swift
Time will only tell
Bodies found adrift
Letters from my cell

Reaction
_hydrus

Be the person i love

Angry demons claw
Chewing through my skin
Bloodied sharpened jaw
Shredding me within

Cannot silence them
Darkened fantasy
Wounded specimen
Lashed to my knees

Devilish thoughts abound
Caged in morbid room
Blackened voices hound
Wailing echoed doom

Death is creeping near
Feeding at demise
Flames engulf the fear
Butchered for my lies

Reaped
_hydrus

Deafened by your stare
Blinded to your noise
I cannot feel your eyes
Your roaring stench destroys

Biting at all senses
Slicing at my wrists
Left to grieve in sadness
Madness does exist

Trapped
_hydrus

Tender lips are gliding
Arched neck placed in hand
Feeling slowly finding
Listening to commands

Wanting just to ravage
Buried in drenched lust
Tamed you have the savage
Moans at every thrust

In charge
_hydrus

Witches kisses
Faintly touch
Slender mistress
Chanting hush

Leaving hexes
Tainted tongues
Wicked weavers
Spells are spun

Casting demons
Familiars prance
Potions brewed
Moonlit dance

Cauldrons stew
Fires blare
Mages capture
Your nightmares

Sirens Treachery
_hydrus

Why must I wait
Prisoner to your needs
Until you feel a burning
Waiting for my quench

Your selfish reward
A deafening silence
For you
I have no thirst

Convenient
_hydrus

Just love

_hydrus

Fire engulfed us
Lips connected
Chances were taken
Deeply addicted

Into our world
Lust still burned
Not enough time
Too much to learn

Passions grew
Love gained
Life was so new
We would then change

Flames flickered
Playing the game
Old habits returned
Reality came

Actions were questioned
All turned dark
Selfish intentions
We lost the spark

An ending so quick
Played for a fool
Painfully sick
Viciously cruel

Over
_hydrus

Sadly you left
I could not reply
Secrets you kept
Simply to hide

Yearning to meet
Silent betrayal
Hidden deceit
Acting so frail

Shattered existence
Terminal lies
Selfish persistence
Loneliness cries

Wretched smile
Taking the fall
Hopeless denial
Ending it all

Confronted
_hydrus

Blame me
For leaving
Trusting us
Deceiving

My fault
Being jaded
Sad truth
Love faded

Runaway
_hydrus

Savage fingers
Hold my hand
Captured by
His demands

Beg and kneel
Quiet roars
Confined spaces
Hidden doors

Love so blind
Dark deceit
Slave to him
Shackled feet

Much despair
Somber sin
Detained lover
Always wins

Game
_hydrus

The taste on my lips linger
Desiring to spread and drink her
Hardened shaft rapidly begs
Devoured by her indulging legs
Warm juices glaze my fingers

Wet
_hydrus

I will
be the
secret
only
you
will
taste
∞

_hydrus

Pretty words
Silly songs
Happy smiles
Somethings wrong
Joyful eyes
Truly hide
Silent fears
Hidden lies

Mask
_hydrus

Your love is my sadness
In a past life we were friends
Jealousies true madness
Incites our malicious end

Punctured
_hydrus

His eyes can write a thousand poems
and only one look will win her heart

Trance
_hydrus

Candles glowing
Petals placed
Scented air
Yearning taste

Spread flesh
Angled form
Wetness drips
Clothes are torn

Hands on girth
Sensuous lips
Fingers pry
Inserted tip

Deep inside
Prints on skin
Passion rides
Forbidden sin

Wanting
_hydrus

Sedated shell a boneless mass
Never awakened taken last
Wanted solely for urge and scent
Willing partner magnificent
Painful tears and dark demands
Sinful fears of the man

Kept
_hydrus

Do not break me without knowing how to put me back together

_hydrus

Thoughts of you
Have not
Ceased
Joyful emptiness
I have reached
Waiting for you
A simple sign
Longing to connect
Show me
You are mine

Tortured
_hydrus

Hands counted down
Sun slept in the west
Joy had been silenced
Spring came to rest

Stolen her breath
Her song quietly wept
My flower now lost
Her beauty now slept

Ageless
_hydrus

Sharpened words
Sliced the smile
Confronted actions
Harsh denials

Clawed backs
Ruptured scars
Broken bottles
Smoke filled bars

Stolen kisses
Swollen eyes
Shattered pieces
Romance dies

Real is painful
Sadness aches
Tonights nightmare
My mistake

Forgiven
_hydrus

A vision of darkness
Enters my room
Draped by her beauty
Buried in gloom
Floating in silence
Inviting my sight
Abducting my senses
Spectral delight
Vacant the voices
Faint are the cries
Vanishing memories
A timeless surprise

Visited
_hydrus

Shining blue ghost
Death scars your wings
Soaring the skies
Diving on sin

Craving our lies
Violently feeding
Nightmares a murder
Gorging and breeding

Binging on fears
Clawing distress
Savagely eaten
Will not confess

Cursed
_hydrus

Words can strangle the innocence out of an honest love
that never learned how to breathe

_hydrus

Consumed
Stretched
And beaten
Devoured flesh
Sobs

Dark Appetite
_hydrus

Unthinkable the notion
Ones vision would be blurred
Drunken in the moment
Unintelligibly slurred

Wondrous attraction
Conveniently mused
Sightless affiliation
Masked in abuse

Inexplicable stranger
Cloaked to conceive
Ripped from my womb
My son was deceived

Calculated
_hydrus

Winged clouds burn the sky
Falling corpses bleed and die
Angels fight on mounted steeds
Demons forge to plant their seed

Swarmed
_hydrus

Whispered words
Inner moans
Hidden touches
Desired groans
Secret places
Passions meet
Disguised kisses
Masked deceit

Shadowed Pleasures
_hydrus

Footsteps are slow
Dread fills the stairs
Inside your soul knows
Fear is everywhere

Anticipation of lust
Desires too much
Taking my bust
Forbidden this touch

Screams fulfill
All wants are met
The animals will
Surrender regrets

Relinquish
_hydrus

I live
knowing
you are not
mine
yet you own
my heart
knowing you
you are the
reason
I am
broken

_hydrus

Drowned
By your madness
Your constant screams
Echo throughout
My soul
Panic you bring
Chaos is your message
Powerless to control
What I cannot see

Anxious
_hydrus

Longing for your body
Savagely intense
Anxious to devour
Slow is the descent

Craving my obsession
Viciously I feast
Drenched in raw emotion
Moaning is the beast

Claimed
_hydrus

Trapped existence
Bound by guilt
Insufficient
Doubt was built

Spying shadows
Separate lives
Deceptive motives
Muffled cries

Locked in sadness
Dishonesty rests
False entrapment
No repent

Knifed
_hydrus

Taste my lost sorrow
Carelessly I bleed
Foolish are my thoughts
Of where things would lead

Lost myself thinking
Living was so pure
Casted for dreaming
Branded insecure

Have I awakened
Nightmares unsealed
Sadly mistaken
New found ordeal

Will I stay lost
Buried with breath
What will it cost
Awaiting my death

Fraud
_hydrus

I am a lost ghost
Trapped in a house
Full of open windows
Nothing to keep me in
Except the fear
Of what
I will find
Beyond

Without Walls
_hydrus

Pay me back as soon as I staple your heart to go fuck yourself

_hydrus

Bottle has found me
Pathetically dazed
Cowardly cringing
Life has gone astray

Drowning to submission
Troubles turn to blur
Coping with admissions
All because of her

Scrambling to forget
Masking pains and ill
Lonesome with regrets
All emotions spill

Flooded sobbing tears
Unable to react
Darkness soon appears
Here goes my final act

Boozed
_hydrus

Binging on your beauty
Thirsting for a taste
Dripping from arousal
Licking every space

How I yearn to drink you
Devouring every sip
Savoring this moment
Lapping luscious lips

Parched
_hydrus

Night smothers the sun
Extinguishing all light
Choking its existence
Brutal in the fight

Scripted duel continues
Flame and ghouls all clash
Defying each surrender
Repeating morbid dance

Regardless of the victor
Stubborn in defeat
Siblings fighting for attention
Never will one cease

The mighty beast submits
Dethroned and left to die
Bowing for the moment
Kneeling just to rise

All Days
_hydrus

Iron doors
Rattled cage
Chained to floors
Untamed rage

Will he kill
Torment pain
Take my will
Leave his stain

Savage hunger
Left to die
My mind wonders
Voiceless cries

Remorse
_hydrus

Iron doors
Rattled cage
Chained to floors
Untamed rage

Will he kill
Torment pain
Take my will
Leave his stain

Savage hunger
Left to die
My mind wonders
Voiceless cries

Remorse
_hydrus

The voices are endless
Misguided and hollow
Where do I run
Who do I follow
Numbing my senses
Counting the time
No more defenses
Losing my mind
Tomorrows a question
The noises tie chains
Seeking redemption
What will remain

No Answers
_hydrus

I am only living to write my own ending

_hydrus

Death is reaping
His laughter chills
Quietly creeping
Chaotic thrills

Invisible demons
Hiding in wait
Ingesting their venom
Poisonous hate

Digesting new victims
Regardless of faith
Feasting unchallenged
Forever my wraith

Feast
_hydrus

A time to kill
Tensions grow
Constant chatter
Losing control
Keep your distance
Do not touch
Living not living
Its fucking too much

Waiting
_hydrus

Ligaments creak
Muscles tear
Cartilage seeps
Bones wear

Earth fills
Worms feast
Maggots spill
Murmured priest

Tears have ended
Time has stopped
Forever forgotten
All was lost

Meaningless
_hydrus

Hands upon my chest
Slowly moving down
Reaching and feeling
Gripping what is found

Pulling on my worth
Veins throbbing in hand
Pulsing feeling warm
Waiting for commands

The Arousal
_hydrus

Swallowed whole
Ripped innocence relayed
Tarnished memories
Constant smearing decay
Judgment passed
Decisions sophomorically made
Guilt has been cast
Nightmares dimly fade

Replay
_hydrus

Paint me with your sin and I will cleanse you with my waste

Toxic   _hydrus

Under the blankets
Begging to receive
Undressed with my illusions
Solely yearning to appease
Forbidden to escape
Lured and tied to please
Throbbing to taste
Grinding to such ease
Filling our thirst
Holding to what is mine
Heated in my bursts
All we have is time

Infinite
_hydrus

You left me already
Did not even let me breathe
Content to abandon
So easy to deceive
Although I miss you
Always waiting to hear
Ignoring my demons
Selfishly wanting you near

Sole
_hydrus

Uncertainty haunts me
Thoughts slowly attack
Panic is inching
Lights turning to black

Silence the voices
So tempted to hide
Questioned existence
Psychotic the ride

Sadistic my future
Shadows coming to claim
Losing my blessings
Cruel is this game

Merciless
_hydrus

Invisible the cages
Trapped in our skin
Craving such rages
Bursting with sin

Hungering to take you
Ravaging the soul
Failing to resist us
Devouring you whole

Sipping every inch
Drowning in your flesh
Spreading as I pinch
Bodies breathlessly mesh

Drenched in pure passion
Heated in embrace
Inside one another
Leaving my trace

A List
_hydrus

Let the dust
From my ashes
Fill you inside
Scorched heart
You left
Gasping
Silent the cries

Crumbled
_hydrus

I dine alone and my thoughts find that humorous

_hydrus

Fear has buried itself
Entering every space
Allowed itself to grow
Replacing all my faith

Full Of
_hydrus

Death is my name
Eagerly sinister
Anguished in pain
Tormenting sadness
Hauntingly sane

My Name
_hydrus

Hear my voice rage
As I tear through the chant
Darkened dungeon cage
Buried beneath the rant

Eternal penance paid
Sentenced simply to rot
Unheavenly judgement made
Settling unholy cost

Eaten through gray skin
Flesh worms eagerly feast
Murders silently made
Hordes gorge the meat

Rock and dirt devour
Never to be found
Forgotten is forever
Slave to the ground

Dread
_hydrus

Lost you to the darkness
Never saw you fall
Blamed for all my weakness
Deaf to drowning calls
Outstretched begging fingers
Hands slowly turning black
Screams echo forgiveness
Fear softly answered back
Demons praise the coward
Angels reap the weak
Soul has named a winner
Victoriously deceased

Abyss
_hydrus

Repressed feelings
Cloaked in smiles
Shrouded guises
Infantile

Childish crushes
Concealed hate
Tempted passion
Hallucinate

Forbidden loves
Clouded past
Separate ways
Aftermath

Frantic words
Accusations
Much mistrust
Devastation

Rumor
_hydrus

Fall in love with the coincidence
that you are an unborn reality
trapped in the beauty
of your ever evolving
unknown

_hydrus

Monster is too simple
This name will not suit
Prejudiced by horrors
Evil birthed at the root

Inhuman your species
Committed you shall
Shameful your deeds
Banished to hell

May you rot from inside
Intestines will foam
Diseased with decay
Brittle the bones

Demons with feast
Eat your soul as you cry
You will meet the beast
And watch yourself die

Purged
_hydrus

Fuck I love your body
The way you fit
between my legs
Eyes that direct
my movements
A tongue that always begs
Never ending hunger
You drip before I feast
Sucking on my fingers
Throbbing just to eat
Never ending passion
Devoured not discreet
Living to consume you
Buried in your heat

Swallowed
_hydrus

Captured glances staring
Undressing me from far
Licking my lips waiting
Moving towards the bar

Slowly he approaches
Slides a hand beneath
Clenching to his fingers
Grinding at his teeth

Dampened sliding motion
Overcame subtle thrill
Clutching my emotions
Bending at all his will

Quickly he retires
Leaving me alate
Bliss has quickly faded
Withdrawing to his date

The Brush
_hydrus

Sand forms
Beneath my toes
As I venture
to the sea

Walking through
Crashing waves
Feeling
The mighty

Outstretched hands
Eyes wide shut
Sunlight gleaming
All on me

Calmy listening
Voices stop
Falling down
I plea

Sadness reigns
Upon my shore
Battles have ceased
To be

One last time
I catch a breath
Eternally
I leave

Departed
_hydrus

Soul full of light
Entered a winning less plight
Disease slowly assailed
Darkness quickly prevailed

Expelled all that was bright
Extinguished the fight
A wound that will not heal
Anguish so real

It should have been me
To leave so suddenly

You left me behind
In a world so unkind

Shattered I walk
To never again talk

You are now free

Alone I must be

Forever
_hydrus

How can you cure me
when I keep infecting myself
with the lies
I am prescribed

_hydrus

Sculpted torment
Crafted to hurt
Jagged insults
Persona Immersed

Purpose simple
Objectives cruel
Strained existence
Sadistic fool

Twisted Pleasure
_hydrus

Gray and black
Adorn my veil
Haunted whispers
Ghostly tales
Reap and scythe
Feast on wine
Dusty ashes
Burned alive
Sins counted
Choices made
Judgement sent
Sentenced fate
Flames devour
Scorching flesh
Decision made
Promises kept

Payment
_hydrus

Stained glass windows
Moonlights dim
Topless shadows
Still with him

Must not dare
Wake his sleep
Judgements harsh
Punishment reaped

Painful nights
Tearful days
Time is broken
Vengeful ways

Hidden
_hydrus

Barren mazes weep
Their captors never sleep
Haunting dreams by day
Trapped thoughts wildly play

Delusions often feast
Forsaken fears must eat
One cannot trust in luck
We are all truly fucked

Mental
_hydrus

Eyes ignite as tensions flow
Allured by light and seductions glow
Sirens chant of luscious deeds
Lips tempt the starving seed

Misleading vixens bloodied swarm
Provokes the embers triggered storm
Engulfed fury of a glamoured spell
The silenced accomplice bids farewell

Vermillion
_hydrus

I sink a hallowed vessel beached upon the lies you cried to be true

_hydrus

Hopeless blackness
Squealing howls
Beckoning grumbles
Maddening scowls
Obscured whimpers
Calling sins
Muttered specters
Grayish skin
Cringing gallows
Ravens Caw
Phantom echoes
Slicing claws

Judgement
_hydrus

Enchanted message
Recoiled thoughts
Triggered feelings
Puzzled wants

Annoyed seduction
Games are played
Simple answers
Obsessed ways

Feed the tempted
Reap the few
Peeved fixation
Charmed recluse

Excited dreamer
Seduced faith
Alarmed deception
Humbled disgrace

Plummet
_hydrus

Dark sadness descends
As I lay in my sorrow
Lost and dismembered
No hope for tomorrow

Blackened dull eyes
Foreboding all thought
Will angels sing loudly
Or the demons just mock

Blood will stream freely
Sweat manically drips
Relinquished from being
The reapers will sip

Cease
_hydrus

Ravens banter
Harass grim sleep
Clamouring yelps
A solace weep

Tears will plunge
Screams foretold
Animus forms
Memories scold

Plagued gestures
Heartbeat crushed
Obscure flutter
Life was hushed

Elapsed
_hydrus

Loves lonesome dagger
Every inch pierced unseen
Left to screaming voices
Barbed edges unclean

Victims to conceit
Echoing self doubt
Greeds true deceit
Bloodied in drought

Frothing assurance
Entrust I did you
Such pain one inflicted
The harm you would spew

Assaulted the slice
Vengeful an ordeal
Abandoned in puddles
To die just to feel

Sacrificed
_hydrus

Never let
your thoughts
drown
in a sea
of your
own
mediocrity

_hydrus

Awakened senses
Lips lightly breached
Snatching moans
Pulsating peach

Gently stroked
Welcoming warmth
Ravaged play
Toying roles

Muscles clench
Bitten skin
Morning bliss
You within

Swollen
_hydrus

Gentle lips caress my neck
Slowly they persist to taste
Our mouths begin to inspect
Hands wander to trace

Stares and sighs exchange
Our bodies quickly tighten
Dampened flesh engages
Internal voices fighting

Devoured skin is breached
A moment held in time
All sorrows are released
Now conquered you are mine

Property
_hydrus

Primal waters drowning fears
Distant echoes shallow tears
Tempered swells chopping storms
Drifting carcass washed ashore

Swept
_hydrus

No one understands
The harsh manifest of lies and manipulation
Twisted words and accusations
May the earth carve you up
Shame your soul
Judged by cruel intentions
Feast on your lack of comprehension
Harness your remains to feed the dogs
You call humanity

Suffer
_hydrus

Creature lingers
Away from light
Tainted misfortune
Consumed by fright

Vigilantly waiting
Anticipates
Looking for weakeness
Life disarray

Hidden in shadows
And in plain sight
Some call friend
Or parasite

Gifted with trust
Hosted to life
Simple pretender
Back will meet knife

Judas
_hydrus

174

I became a figment of your past the moment you did not accept reality.

Submissive play I invite
Tender lips to entice
Vengeful tactics your demise
Observe your master
Realize
Truth now shaken
Lost control
All has changed
You lost your soul

New Rules
_hydrus

Crimson embers pale and warm
Enticing visits from feeding swarms
Spring streaks sketching the sky
Autumn meets only to die
Melted puddles heaped in snow
Willows angered as they grow
harmonic music one may think
Natures death all will drink

Eroded
_hydrus

A sudden vision and you appeared
A past reminder you felt so near
I couldnt move or catch my breath
The sudden pain that you had left
It felt so real I had to wake
The loss of you was far too great

Bare
_hydrus

Secret illusions cloud my nights
Strained temptations haunt the light

Intimate pleasures disguised allure
Committed relations blatantly cruel

Implied affections plague intent
Obscure delusions masked repent

Shameful perception fraudulent path
Innocence scorned malicious my wrath

Malice
_hydrus

Fallen angels
Bellowed horns
Twisting shackles
Dressed in thorns

Gods have clamored
Screamed in vein
Passing judgment
Numb disdain

Soulless vagrants
Ascents denied
Watching darkness
Cloud their eyes

Mortals soundly
Learn of fate
Earthly deeds
Incriminate

Heaved corpses
Gasping wails
Collapsed hope
Forgiveness failed

Heathens gasp
Await the lords
Tumbling down to
Hungry hordes

Fools belief
Redemptions call
Cleansed in fire
As they fall

Plunge
_hydrus

You protect me only to watch me break

_hydrus

Storms buried
Me at sea
Escaping my
Own destiny
Swallowed soul
In disarray
Left to drown
In my decay

Smothered madness
Sloshing waves
Ending sadness
Sinking grave

Helpless voyage
Silenced crushed
Life was too much
Tears were hushed

Returned
_hydrus

184

Solace holds a grudge
Redemptions broken skill
Avenged mistakes will judge
Extractions you fulfill
Evils vengeful crush
Retorted fist must kill
Jealousies secret hush
A prisoner of his will

Escape
_hydrus

Malicious viper
So serpentine
Barbed toxins
Injected clean

Spreading venom
Unknown surprise
Secreting poisons
Cruelly paralyzed

Camouflaged feelings
Slithering skills
Friend to all victims
Simply bitten for thrills

Fangs
_hydrus

Sun rises as the corpses lie
Wooden crosses paint the sky
Blades of grass tear into me
Shredded masses bleed to sea
Waves reveal a stench of hate
Torn to pieces
Simply mutilate
Fallen angels drowned in sand
Metal angered by the touch of man

Slaughter
_hydrus

I catch my breath
As it escapes my heart
Conceded departure
Simply torn apart

Counting the clouds
As they shield your flight
Struggling in silence
A dreadful spite

Abstractively hollow
Purpose misplaced
Distant the voices
Erased of your trace

The moment will pass
Miseries will cease
Waiting in sorrow
Sadness in peace

Torment
_hydrus

I never knew what it meant to fall
                    yet it became a habit we felt accustomed to

                    _hydrus

Spring awaits at dormant doors
Barred existence earthly roars
Nomadic silence everclear
Masked delusions chronic fears
Barred reclusion new decrees
Societies mantra live diseased

Times
_hydrus

Emptiness is mocking
Choking my veins
Slowing all healing
Draining the sane

Space that you held
Voided all pain
Wretched life begging
Feelings not claimed

Cold vacant body
Boasting rebuke
Depleted instructions
Pointless in truth

Gapingly searching
Awkwardely vain
Ransacked excursion
Falsely mundane

Conflict
_hydrus

Twisted storms
Bitterly feud
Within my heart
Despair exudes

Tortured panics
Engulfed rage
Sickly manic
Estranged escape

Mindless banters
Reap my wounds
Kneeling judgements
Stigma looms

Fate has married
Death to me
Avenging alters
Sweet misery

.

Ceremony
_hydrus

Cringing shame forgotten
Apologies of the sin
Mercies own discretion
Submissions from within

Chastened outcry lulled
Repenting banished cry
Shamed deluded skulls
Surrendered one must die

Revoked confessions burn
Rescinded of your birth
Voided of transgressions
Immersed in tainted worth

Pardons for such actions
Betrayals all will bleed
Accused of my extinction
Abandoned screams will plead

Vindicate
_hydrus

Distant hunger
Barren grounds
Withered thunder
Absent sounds
Ashes wait
Incoming rains
Soak the soul
Wash my pain

Tears
_hydrus

∞

Thank you to all who have embarked on this
journey with me...
through all of the darkness and some of the
light.
You will always have a place in my black heart.

Humbled
_hydrus

C./G.

Thank You

Beauty of whatever kind, in its supreme development,
invariably excites the sensitive soul to tears.

-Edgar Allan Poe

Also by _hydrus

ENDvisible

A collection of poems about the endless feeling of being invisible while
going through the emotions and sometimes
cruelties of life. Illustrated by the
author's own photography, this book guides us through grief, loss and love
in a dark and inspiring way typical to how
Hydrus's writing helps us cope with reality.

AwakEND

Tarots cards, much like poems, have the ability to paint a vivid picture of
what once was or what could be. They delve into the subtleties that we all
carry within ourselves and the secrets that make us who we are.

AwakEND is an immersion into the world of tarot and its mysteries.Read
it one way, then another, and let the words guide you into the meaning of
each card. Allow chance and curiosity to accompany you on this incredi-
ble journey and let your heart awaken to hope even after having thought
everything was lost...
And who knows what secrets you might find out about yourself...

About The Author

Anonymous poet, photographer and artist,
Hydrus documents through his poems the darkness and the
glimmers of life taunting us when we are in the shadows, as
well as many of the little things which make a
colossal impact on who we are.

Connect with hydrus:

Website: www.hydruspoetry.com
Instagram: instagram.com/hydruspoetry
Facebook: https://www.facebook.com/hydruspoetry

Answer: Just be you

Write your Soul

_hydrus

Made in United States
Orlando, FL
20 April 2022

17031395R00129